JANE CAMPION

THE POWER OF THE DOG

ASSOULINE

Deliver my soul from the sword; my darling from the power of the dog.

PSALM 22:20

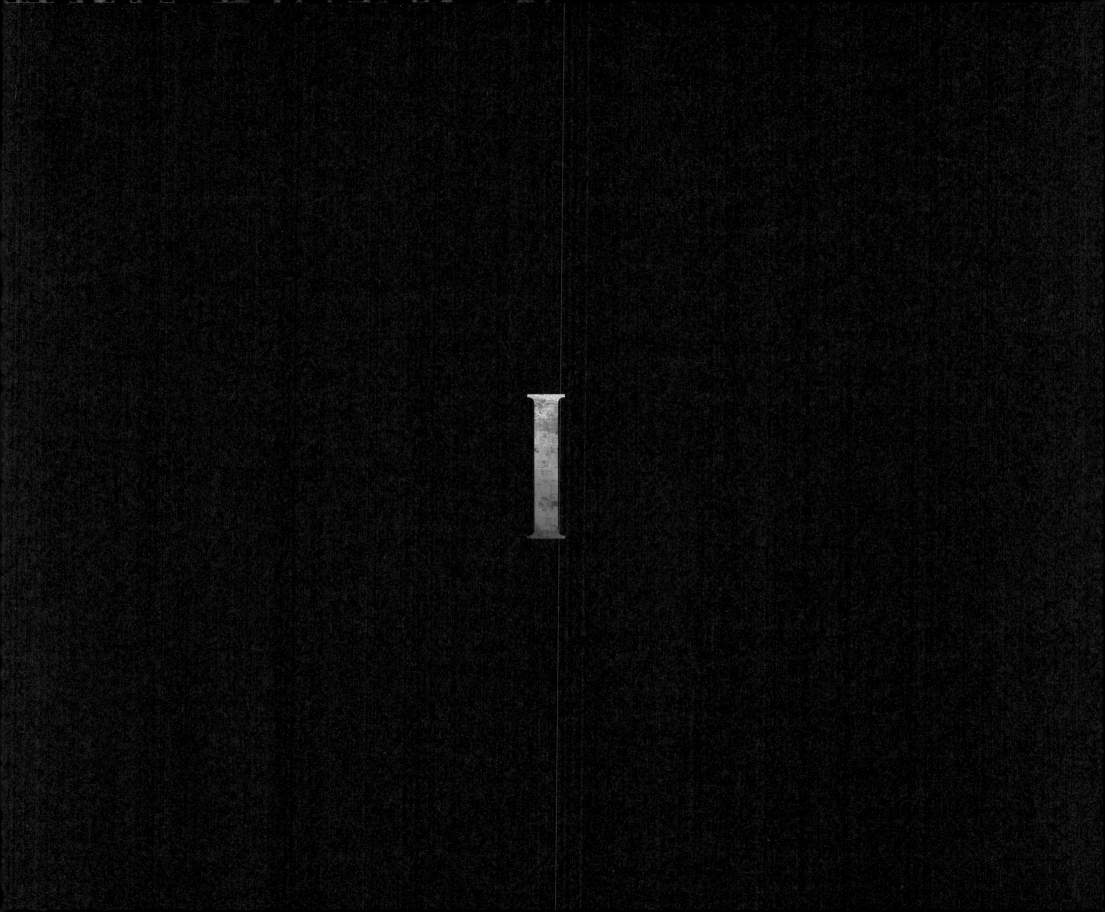

I

INTRODUCTION

Jane Campion

The book *The Power of the Dog,* by Thomas Savage, was sent to me in early 2017 by my dad's wife, Judith, who is a great reader. I read it and loved it. Over the next weeks, Savage's story haunted me. Images kept coming, and I found myself drawn to the characters, the themes, the story. I asked my agent if she could explore the rights, and I told my friend producer Tanya Seghatchian (*Cold War*) about the book. She read it and loved it too. The rights, however, were not available; they belonged to the Canadian producer Roger Frappier. He was going to Cannes and so was I. We met in the Carlton for coffee. When I saw him, I laughed: we looked so similar—silver-haired, black-rimmed glasses, the same height—we could have been brother and sister.

The writing of the script was rapid, with Tanya's help and companionship and the feedback of Roger and fellow producers Iain Canning and Emile Sherman. But with the directing, for a long time I hesitated at the cliff edge. My dreams were of fear. In one, I was riding a spirited black horse bent on his and my destruction as we zigzagged down an impossibly narrowing cliff pass that was too tight, finally, for the horse's hooves. Retreat was impossible, death seemed inevitable.

The novel had deep and true bones, and a depth that demanded complete immersion. I knew I had to dive, but how? A friend suggested dreamwork with Kim Gillingham. That felt right. My psyche was clearly triggered, and with Kim's help, the further I went in, the more rewarded I was, as the themes had a way of peeling themselves open, always deepening, always surprising. So, like a lover, I eventually offered my whole self to Savage's magnificent story. I let it sweep me up. I saw the lover in Phil as well as his sharp, judging eye and cruel tongue. I saw the importance and strength of each of the characters to the story and the bewildering pain of Phil's sexuality lived furtively and always in the past, until Peter arrived and brought it all up again.

This book is an attempt to share the story in photographs as well as insight into the vitalizing and intense collaborations that transformed the novel into a film.

May 21, 2018: Jane and Roger met in Cannes.

SYNOPSIS

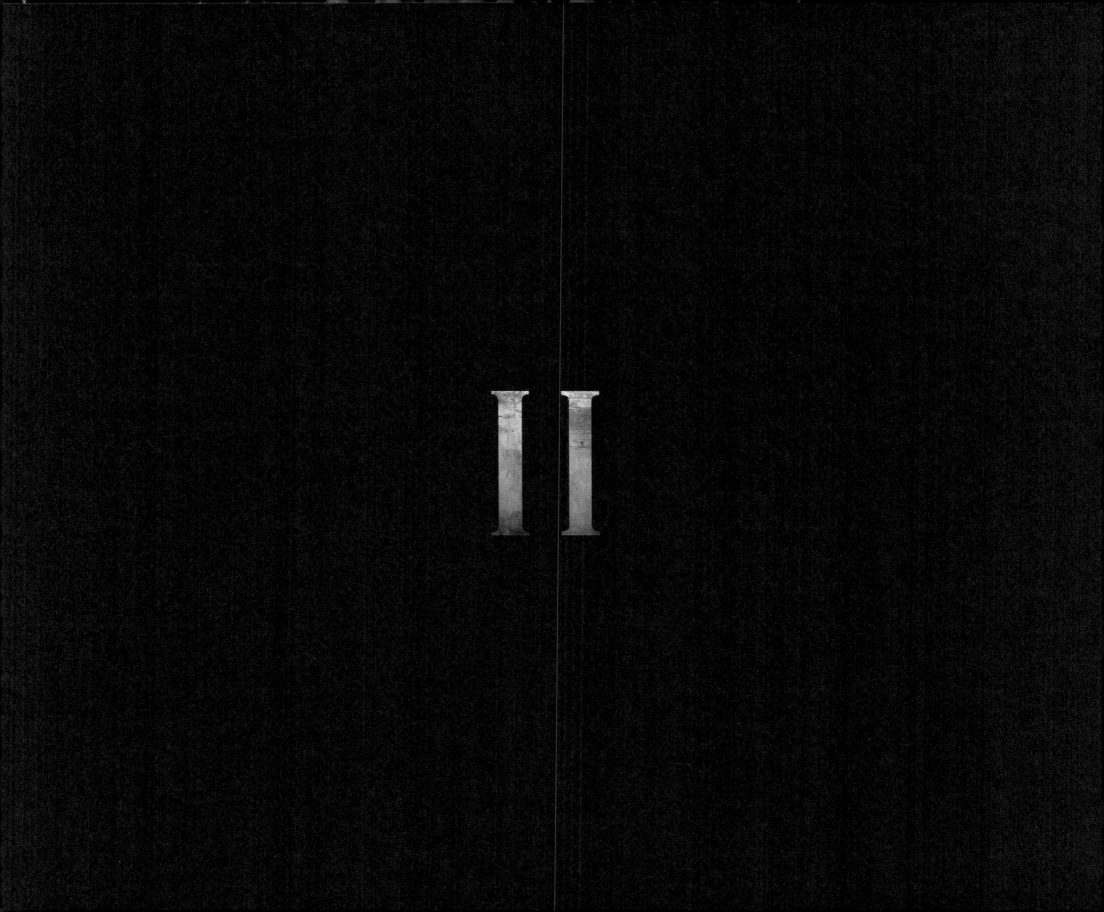

SYNOPSIS

Severe, pale-eyed, handsome, Phil Burbank is brutally beguiling: a gifted man trapped by grief and his own disallowed desire. While his younger brother, George, harbors hopes that tend towards society, Phil's connections are to nature. He sees shapes in the hillside that are invisible to others; he can castrate a bull with two swift slashes of his knife; he swims naked in the river, smearing his body with mud. He is a cowboy as raw as his hides: all of Phil's romance, power and fragility are derived from the land.

The year is 1925. The Burbank brothers are wealthy ranchers in Montana. Over the years George has grown immune to Phil's charisma, liberally lapped up by the cowhands who accompany them, and is unmoved by Phil's tales of their long-dead mentor, Bronco Henry.

At the Red Mill restaurant on their way to market, the brothers meet Rose, the widowed proprietress, and her impressionable son, Peter. Phil behaves so cruelly he drives them both to tears, reveling in their hurt and rousing his fellow men—all except George—to a chorus of laughter.

George comforts Rose, then returns to marry her.

Rose—beautiful, gentle, humble, generous—teaches George to dance in the middle of the mountains. "You are marvelous, Rose," her new husband declares, a tear rolling down his cheek. So marvelous, it seems, that she must be destroyed by George's resentful brother, Phil. Snowbound in a gold dress, the new Mrs. Burbank nervously hosts the Governor and his wife for dinner. Asked to play the piano for them, as she once did for the moving pictures, Rose is paralyzed with fear—and Phil's campaign of mental torment has its first success.

Peter has been sent to boarding school. He comes home for the summer to find his mother hiding liquor bottles under her pillow. A rabbit he dissects might stand for his forensic attitude towards life, and his growing medical knowledge becomes a hidden source of strength.

As Phil swings between fury and manipulation, he acquires a noxious, centrifugal power. His taunting of Rose takes an eerie form: he hovers at the edges of her vision, whistling the tune she can no longer play. His mockery of Peter's effeminacy is more overt, amplified by the laughter of Phil's cowhand disciples. After Peter happens on Phil as he communes with the memory of Bronco Henry in a sacred spot by the river, Phil appears to take the boy under his wing. Is this latest gesture a softening that leaves Phil exposed, or a plot twisting further into menace?

We're told that Phil was a brilliant student of classics at Yale; his return to the family ranch may have been due to Bronco, the man who once kept him alive by lying "body against body in a bedroll." Phil's loyalty to the long-dead cowboy remains fierce enough to inflect everything he does with reverence—and leaves him vulnerable to echoes of romance.

Phil and George, Rose and Peter, George and Rose, Rose and Phil: our attention shifts from one pair of characters to another, as if they were the intertwined strands in Phil's plaited rope. Eventually it settles on the unexpected duo of Peter and Phil, who circle one another, Phil vulnerable to echoes of romance, Peter enflamed to save.

Gaby Wood is the director of the Booker Prize Foundation.

THE FILM

III

"To the outside world, Phil is somebody who's utterly in control of his world and the people in it. But there's this thing that's out of his control that society has denied him. That's part of why he's so savage about his circumstance and the people in it. It's twisted him."

BENEDICT CUMBERBATCH, *Phil Burbank*

"In the beginning, what motivates George are very basic, simple things—keeping time, keeping schedule, keeping everything running and operating. That's his role on the ranch—and also, subtly, sweeping up after Phil and whatever mess he makes."

JESSE PLEMONS, *George Burbank*

"Anything feminine whatsoever is an affront to Phil, and in comes Rose, who is as feminine of a figure as you can find. Phil is scared he's losing his brother, which he sort of is. Underneath all of that petulant, childish anger, he's scared of losing him."

JESSE PLEMONS

PHIL

Twenty-five years ago, where were
you, Georgie boy? I'll tell you—
a chubby know-nothing, too dumb
to get through college.

PHIL
My goodness, I wonder what little lady
made these?

PETER
I did, actually, sir.

"Phil is always alert, careful not to drink too much in case he reveals himself to the cowhands. It's clear in the book that he had sex with some of the seasonal workers, which was dangerous. At that time homosexuality was condemned and sodomy a crime punishable with one to twenty years' prison time. That's a very bitter thing, because to him his lust feels true and right but society is saying he's a deviant. Phil is clever, a scholar, a good speaker, a great story spinner, a skilled musician, but he's ambivalent towards a 'sassiety' that would persecute him. Phil never uses the house bath, preferring to smear his body with mud by the riverbank. When George finds him sulking in the barn before the fated dinner party, Phil refuses to clean up or play host. 'What will I say?,' asks George. 'Tell them I stink and I like it.' "

JANE CAMPION, *writer/director*

"What I do with every role and did with Rose is kind of a therapy between me and the person I'm playing. Rose is a very old part of myself—a very insecure person who could easily be gaslit. She is sensitive and easily affected by others, and I related to that in my younger years. It was a very odd place to revisit and put myself back in a vulnerable position when you have been hurt very badly."

KIRSTEN DUNST, *Rose*

"What's so powerful about Peter
is that you don't want to judge him.
He's got so much more going on
beneath him that drives him as a human
being. He's such a genuine, beautiful
soul, and he doesn't do anything to
conform to people's judgments."

KODI SMIT-McPHEE, *Peter*

"Nostalgia is a theme in the film and so relevant to today. It's still present in our politics, in our life, this nostalgia for a purer, more perfect time. Phil builds a shrine to it. Here it's very deeply connected with what he's hiding, what he's repressed."

EMILE SHERMAN, *producer*

GEORGE
What you said about her boy tonight,
Phil, made her cry.

COWHANDS
C'mon, Phil, there is something
there, right?

PHIL
Not if you can't see it, there ain't.

PHIL

Give her [Rose] a chance and she'll be after some dollar for Miss Nancy's college fees—
If it's a piece of ass you're after, fatso, I'm damn sure you can get it without a license.

"I like to think that Mrs. Lewis is
the conduit between the parents—
the Old Gent and the Old Lady—and
the two brothers."

GENEVIEVE LEMON, *Mrs. Lewis*

GEORGE
The Old Lady would feel what
one Mrs. Burbank would feel for
another Mrs. Burbank.

PHIL
You goddamned whore,
you hear me? You dirty
flat-faced bitch.

"To Phil, Rose is a woman pretending. He's had enough of that in his life. His mother is that, and now he's seeing his brother sucker punched by Rose's looks and he can't abide her. Most importantly, in losing his brother, he's losing his connection to his true self, which is his past and his relationship with Bronco Henry. In seeing their union, he has a subconscious well of pain and jealousy stirred up that he has to keep hidden from the world."

BENEDICT CUMBERBATCH

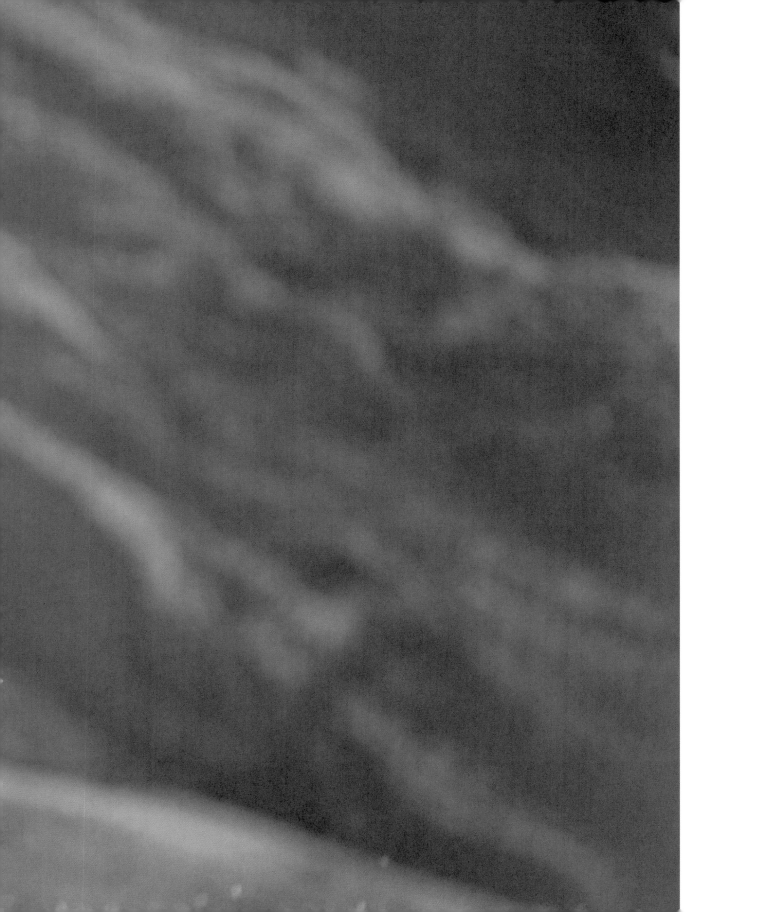

GEORGE
I just wanted to say how nice it is
not to be alone.

IN LOVING MEMORY
BRONCO HENRY
FRIEND
1854 - 1904.

PHIL
Tell them the truth—that I stink
and I like it!

ROSE
That's too good for me.
I only know tunes.

"I avoided speaking to Benedict on set. And for
the dinner scene, I didn't really talk to any
people—just so I could have that feeling where
you have a lump in your throat."

KIRSTEN DUNST

GEORGE
Play the one I like.

ROSE
What one?

GEORGE
Why, the one about the Gypsy.

"Phil becomes somebody who hates the world before it can hate him. He has a desire to control chaos and master all aspects of his life. It's both empowering and crippling. He's been masking so much for so long he truly has become the hardened ranchman of many skills and much unacknowledged pain."

BENEDICT CUMBERBATCH

"Phil realizes that Peter embraces who he is in a way that Phil never could, and he admires and envies him for it. Even though they go into this mission connivingly and maliciously, they actually find somewhat of an unexpected safe haven with each other. That's one of the layers that stands out so deeply and impacts me. But in the end Peter plays Phil's game far better than Phil. He's met his match."

KODI SMIT-McPHEE

PETER
It's Phil, isn't it? He's cold.

ROSE
He's a man, just another man.

Phil doesn't wash very often, so his visit to the river is more like a baptism than a bath or shower. It's reconnecting with who he is as an animal and sexually. It's where he's at his most free. He allows himself to drift back to the romance of the past, to fantasize over Bronco and what that relationship was."

BENEDICT CUMBERBATCH

"At one point we see a distinct switch in the way that Phil treats Peter, and he almost seems to take a liking to him, take him under his wing, want to teach him how to run the ranch as a masculine male would, just like all the other cowboys. Peter goes along with it, which I think would cause a lot of fear in anyone observing that— the audience or Rose. But I think Peter is always one step ahead."

KODI SMIT-McPHEE

PETER

You want me, Mr. Burbank?

PHIL

I don't see any Mr. Burbank here. I'm Phil.
Peter, we kinda got off on the wrong foot.

PETER

Did we, sir?

PHIL

Forget the "sir"stuff. That can happen to people,
you know, people who get to be good friends.
Well, you know what?

PETER

What—what, Phil?

PHIL

Now, you see, you did it—you called me Phil.
I'm gonna finish this rope and give it to you
and teach you how to use it.
Sort of a lonesome place out here, Pete, unless
you get in the swing of things.

PHIL
Just sitting there, you're soaking up all the riding
know-how you'll ever need, then some. That
saddle belonged to Bronco Henry, the greatest
horseman I ever knew. But Bronco, when he
looked, what do you suppose he saw?

PETER
A running dog.

PHIL
The hell you see it just now?

"Phil continues to be surprised by Peter—his defiance in the return walk between the tents and that he sees things in the way that only Phil or Bronco Henry did, like the dog on the hill. I think that is the moment when he starts to look at the boy in a very different light, in a way that permits an understanding and an empathy. It's Phil utterly revealed, and there's something vulnerable about it."

BENEDICT CUMBERBATCH

"Phil is obsessed with 'Who can see this?'
Because he's the only one who can see it. And
it's not just a question of visual perception.
Really he's asking, 'Who can see me? Who
can see the real me?' The 'me' that lies
underneath his layers of pretense, which are
incredibly powerful, aggressive, strong layers.
He protects and hates those parts inside
him at the same time. He desperately
wants to be seen."

EMILE SHERMAN

ANTHRAX

gating medical world. No one guessed at their true nature for a long time. They were looked upon as crystals, as fibrin formations, as curiosities, of no etiological importance, and having no connection with the disease.

Anthrax is a disease of animals communicable to man. It finds its way into the human blood stream through cuts or breaks in the skin from man's handling the hide of a diseased animal.

Infection.—If one has a suspicion or knows that the case before him is anthrax, if there is not a local lesion, as is frequently the case in man (Fig. 1.), and desires to confirm his diagnosis, all that is necessary is to draw a few drops of blood either from the lesion or a vein and examine it microscop... introduce it under the skin of a mouse ... rabbit, and the animal will ... within twenty-four hours ... time and forty-eight ... of inoculation ... to work ...

PETER

Mother, you don't have to do this.
I'll see you don't have to do it.

ROSE
I don't want that. I don't want
him to be with Phil at all.

PHIL

Bronco said a man is made up
from patience and the odds
against him.

You, too strong? He got that
wrong, you poor kid. Things will
work out for you yet.

"Phil's campaign of psychological torture is so overt and cruel that Rose feels ashamed to bring it up to George. After all, it's their house and she feels it's up to her to somehow try and accept George's brother. Yet Phil's unrelenting efforts to humiliate her make Rose turn to alcohol to try and survive. Before long she is drinking towards a crisis."

KIRSTEN DUNST

MRS. LEWIS

Phil doesn't want anyone else to
have them [the hides]. He waits till
there's a pile and burns the lot.
It's a terrible smell all day.

"I think when Rose hears about
the Native Americans and the hides being
burned for no reason, there is some
unconscious soul connection of how they've
been mistreated and how she's being
mistreated. That moment when you can't
defend and fight for yourself, it's easier to fight
for other people. Rose has so much rage, but
she doesn't know where to put it."

KIRSTEN DUNST

PETER
Why would she do that, Phil? Why?
She knew we needed the hides.

PHIL
Because she was drunk!
Pie-eyed! Stewed!

PETER
Phil, I've got rawhide to finish
the rope.

PHIL
You've got it? What you doing
with rawhide?

IN LOVING MEMORY
BRONCO HENRY

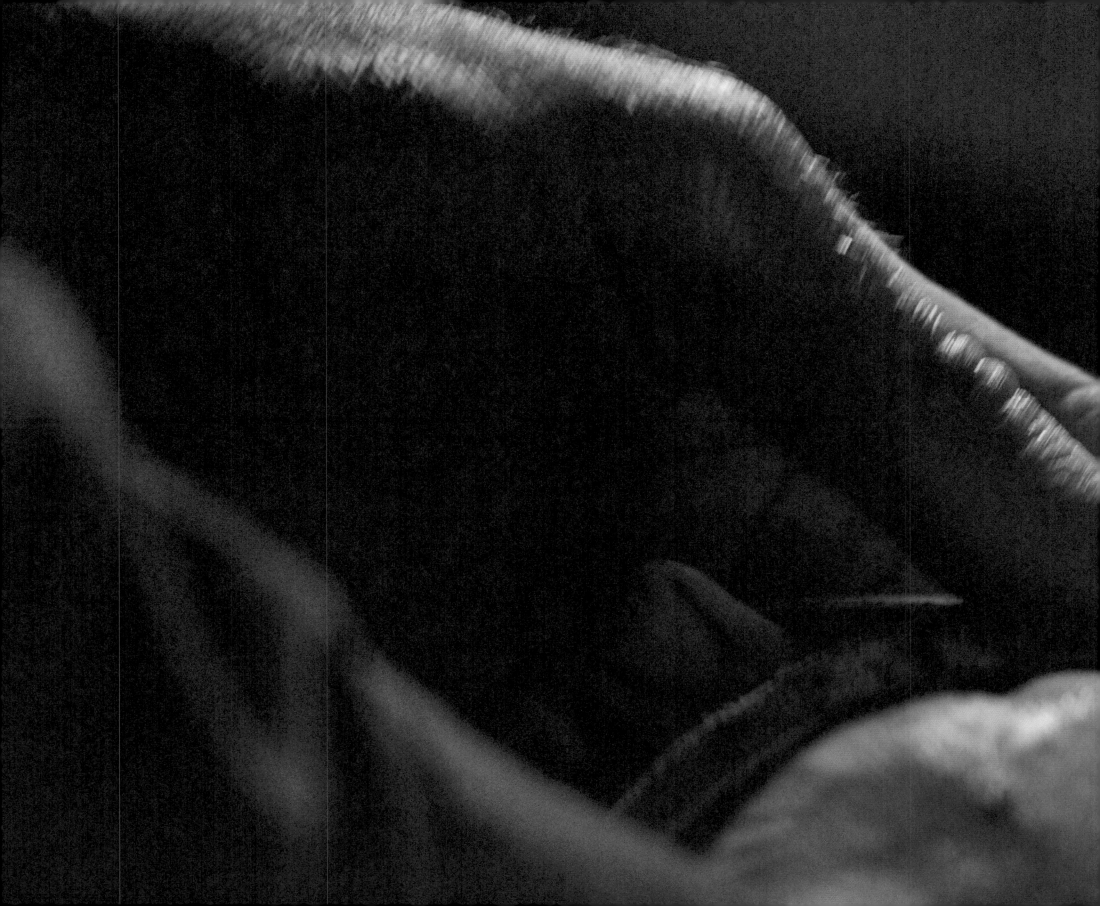

PETER
Naked?

PHIL
Where's the boy?

"I think *The Power of the Dog* is fundamentally about human nature and how the world we live in too often forces us to hide our true self under layers of artifice. What we see in the film is a series of stealthy revelations about the true nature of two very strong characters who have much more in common than either of them first realizes or would care to admit. Phil and Peter both share an unusual ability to look beyond the surface of a situation and see the deeper truth underneath. At one level, that's symbolized by the shadow dog on the hill that only they can see, but also both are characters who are hiding their pain and their yearning from the rest of the world. I think that's what makes the film resonate in the way it does. We all know what it is to hold strong emotions secret in our hearts, and the true power of Jane's film comes from the way she strips away all the layers of artifice to reveal a surprising vulnerability and humanity underneath. At this point, what we're really looking at is the human condition—and in terms of creating art there is nothing more universal or more resonant."

TANYA SEGHATCHIAN, *producer*

MAKING THE FILM

IV

"My friendship with Tanya began about fifteen years ago when she pulled my script *Bright Star* out of a rubbish bin at the British Film Institute and insisted on funding the film in a 'we do this or I go' gauntlet. Tanya's fierce intelligence is matched by an endearing love for the possibility of film really shifting consciousness as well as a true personal kindness. I love her for her passion. It helps me stretch to my full potential just knowing I have a friend colluding with the many foul and fair winds that impact productions. Tanya and I are emotional in a way I don't experience with men in our industry; we have sobbed together at dinner tables and later laughed hilariously at our intensity. Tanya champions mystery over logic and has a particular capacity to embolden artistic risks, always sharing her own honest opinion. We bore the creative wonders and miseries of the production, from the adapting of the novel to the final mixing, speaking remotely when the pandemic separated us."

JANE CAMPION

LOOKING FOR "THE DOG"

Tanya Seghatchian

HOW IT ALL BEGAN...

Jane and I had been looking for a feature to make together for over a decade. We first met in 2007, when I ran the National Film Funds in the UK, after I'd read her script for *Bright Star,* about the poet Keats and his love for Fanny Brawne. I was reading the script in bed and was so swept up by their love story that I wrote a love letter to Jane and her producer Jan Chapman, offering to lend my support. When Jane came to London, we became friends. She invited me to stay with her in Australia for Christmas, and we began to find ways to spend time together and share ideas, even though we lived on opposite sides of the world—a fact we didn't allow to get in the way.

Ten years later she suggested I read the novel *The Power of the Dog,* by Thomas Savage. I read it in one sitting, struck by how nuanced and rich the book was and by Savage's evocation of an unfamiliar American West. Here was an intricately woven psychodrama, with strong yet fragile characters looking for love, whose complex passions were so precisely plotted that the ingenious, chilling ending crept up and caught me completely unaware.

It also felt curiously modern for a book written in the 1960s and set in the 1920s and, with a depiction of Phil's parasitical, toxic relationship to femininity at its center, a particularly exciting book for Jane to adapt.

We were surprised Thomas Savage was not better known, and later found out that the book had been in and out of option but nobody had managed to get it across the line, even with Paul Newman coveting the role. It was only later that I realized the taut plot that makes the story so instantly attractive is only half the challenge. To make a film that fulfills the true promise of the book was always going to demand a screenwriter and a director who would lean in to the subtle, dark and profoundly emotional undercurrents that fuel the ambivalent relationships between the main players.

Jane has a sensitivity for finding hidden notes and intensifying sensuality. One of her real gifts is making invisible emotions visible. So even though Bronco Henry, who plays such a pivotal role in Phil's memory, is long dead and absent from the present, I knew she would find a way into Phil's psyche that was cinematic. She knows instinctively how to augment scenes only partially described in the book, pinpointing themes and emotional gaps to explore more deeply, using images to highlight desire and make it come alive. The pivotal seduction scene in the barn is a good example of how she creates a mood and tension that are as mysterious and contradictory as the relationship they depict.

THE RESEARCH TRIP

Annie Proulx's afterword to the novel of *The Power of the Dog* was an insightful introduction to Thomas Savage, and given that Jane and I are both such fans of her writing, I wrote to Annie to ask if we might visit her in the States. She invited us to her home for lunch, and after spending a morning dissecting the book with her over crab claws, we felt more confident in our approach.

I had also approached Alan Weltzien, an English professor at the University of Montana Western, who was writing a biography about Savage and how he continually re-inhabited Montana, often as a scene of gender protest. Alan was on a mission to bring our brilliant forgotten novelist to the attention of a wider public, and enthusiastically offered to escort us around "Savage Country." We met him in the town of Dillon (on which the Herndon of our story is based), and with a biographer's eye, he walked us through places that had been the inspiration for Savage's fiction. Alan arranged for us to have dinner with Thomas's nephew Sandy and Sandy's wife, Jeannie, who gave us their family photo album, which included photos of the man they thought was Savage's Bronco Henry, and also of Thomas's step-uncle. Jeannie confided that Rose's story mirrored elements of her own: that, like Rose, she had felt a sense of powerlessness and loneliness when she married, and that it took a while for her to find her feet. We were very moved by her honest account of what Rose might have felt, marrying into a family where the business of the ranch would always have primary importance over any feelings of isolation.

Alan took us to see the plot where the original Savage ranch house had been built, and we also saw the remains of the Savage family home. We had so wanted to shoot in Montana, but the ranch house was much smaller than the mansion Savage described in the book, and we realized then that we were going to have to build what we needed from scratch, but

also that we would have to do it somewhere with more production infrastructure. Ironically, it became clear quickly that the most cost-effective and seasonally appropriate location was going to be in New Zealand.

Just before we left Montana, Alan took us on a hilltop picnic above the old Savage ranch. As we were driving away, Jane looked back across the hills and saw the shape or the outline of a dog in the landscape. As soon as she pointed it out, Alan and I both saw it too, and we stood there watching it stare back at us. Jane photographed it and took it as a sign from Thomas Savage, "a kind of kiss," she said, as if he were entrusting the story to her.

COLLABORATION

People are curious about our creative collaboration. It really began a long time ago. I think when we first met, she immediately saw who I was. That I wanted more connection, and that she could give me that. *Sweetie* and *An Angel at My Table* and *The Piano* had all changed my perspective on cinema and on life, so maybe it was ordained that, if we met, we would connect deeply. She was willing to let me in, and we quickly cut through the small talk. Over time, we have evolved a rare symbiotic power, which both brings us confidence and is founded on mutual respect, trust and intelligence. It is very empowering. I suspect that at root we're both hopeless romantics—but with an ability to not take ourselves too seriously. Ultimately, Jane is singular, disciplined and wholly original, and I'm fiercely protective of her vision and feed it when I can. I appreciate that she lets me contribute creatively, and there is no fear of destabilizing her process because she is experienced and she is strong. We are very honest with each other, and we use humor and intelligence to keep us together and underpin the hard work and commitment to the film.

THE ADAPTATION

Jane's adaptation was striking in how she crafted the central story. Her first draft was bold about what to keep and what to cut. She didn't want to make a saga. The novel lays out Rose's and Phil's backstories in much greater depth than the script, but Jane wanted to enter the story at a point of imminent change, with just enough lead-up to justify the outcome. A dance between our four leads, brothers Phil and George and Rose and Peter, a mother and son, who circle each other and seem to move inexorably towards a surprising but inevitable end.

She knew early on that the ranch and its landscape shaped our characters and always wanted location and atmosphere to heighten their claustrophobia and loneliness. She absorbed the symbols and signs and elevated moments, rendering them poetically and cinematically to haunt the story. Whether it's the "dog" on the hill or the braided rope or the ghostly presence of Bronco that remains so present in Phil's imagination and repression, she uses these elements to reveal the real, soulful Phil, who's buried so deep that it's a miracle he comes back to life and to love one last time.

Jane is very conscious of succinct dialogue, structure and pace, and can apply a mathematician's precision to her screenwriting from the outline onwards.

Jane is quick to put everyone at ease. She is self-deprecating and inclusive. She gets the best out of everyone around her by making people feel safe and supported and acknowledging they all have an essential part to play. We ran a small, tight and mobile-free set to ensure everyone was focused.

Jane always wanted a sense of dread and desire entwined from the outset. Phil's meanness and cruelty are the flip side to his powerful charisma. We needed him to be domineering on-screen but also seduce us at the same time. He's a Renaissance man trapped in this crude lifestyle, whilst his memories give him comfort and something profound to focus on. Her focus was always on "Phil the monster," who is also "Phil the lover," a brilliant man yet a spiteful child. Phil the rancher and academic star could possibly have become president, but who never left home or found anyone to share his adult life with aside from his dissatisfied younger brother, George. These were the core elements of Phil's character that Jane took to conjure the complex, menacing character Benedict portrays so brilliantly.

I think more than most films *The Power of the Dog* is a very complete film. The world these characters inhabit feels fully realized, but it is also hermetically sealed. Could any of these people escape their fate? In theory, yes, but in fact Jane has set up a world that has the Burbank ranch at its center and our characters are all locked into its orbit. When there is disagreement, there is no question of running away. Everyone is locked into a danse macabre until an end that feels as surprising as it is inevitable.

THE POWER OF THE DOG

by Thomas Savage

Screenplay by Jane Campion

Front and back covers of the internal script used by the cast.
From left: *Untitled (Dog),* by Giacomo Brunelli, 2006.
Sin nombre, by Harold Mendez, 2018.

THE NOVEL

From left: Thomas Savage at a book reading; Thomas Savage, author of *The Power of the Dog* (1967).

"When a story really excites me, I sit up. I kept coming back to *The Power of the Dog*. It haunted me. That is always a sign it's got more. The challenge is, what am I going to do that no one else will do?"

JANE CAMPION

"When Jane's agent called me to ask about the rights, I nearly fell off my chair. I've been a great fan of Jane's since *An Angel at My Table*. I have such great respect and admiration for her. We had a rendezvous at Cannes, spoke for an hour and I really felt that we were on the same wavelength about the book and making this movie. I'd been developing the project for eight years, and I was never pleased with the way it was coming up. Suddenly I felt, after all that time, that it's come to the right place with the right person."

"You cannot imagine my joy after developing the project for all those years to see a vision of the film fulfilled to its utmost potential because of the great talent of Jane Campion, including her incredible adaptation of the book and the sensitivity of her direction, the amazing performance of the actors and the quality and contributions of all the artistic crew. It is a rare moment in the life of a producer, and I cherish it."

ROGER FRAPPIER, *producer*

SEE-SAW FILMS

"I've been working with Jane for nearly a decade now. It really is an extraordinary experience to work with her. You learn all the time. She's not like any other director or writer or creator that we work with. Jane is not a transactional person in her life, and she's not a transactional creative. She wants to come from a place of genuine human connection."

"So the bedrock of the relationship is trust. And that trust manifests itself all the way through the production process. My ambition is always to return the trust to her by ensuring that we are supporting and enabling her to realize her vision."

EMILE SHERMAN

"At See-Saw we're always looking for projects from incredibly talented filmmakers with a distinctive vision. Unarguably, Jane is one of the most talented filmmakers in the history of cinema. So it's a real honor that we get to work with her on this film."

"Jane was very passionate about Thomas Savage's novel. She completely fell in love with the book and wanted to honor his storytelling. The film unpicks and investigates the construct of masculinity, and it does that in a very unique way."

IAIN CANNING, *producer*

CASTING

"Phil Burbank is one of the all-time great characters of American fiction. He's so complicated, and even as cruel, mean and unkind as he often is, he's also a man with intense feeling. He's a lover, but he can only love safely in the past."

"Benedict is an extraordinarily talented guy. He is very honest and focused and also a mimic who does accents amazingly well. He and I started working together eight months before we began. I knew whoever was going to play Phil Burbank would have to do a lot of work to be convincing as a character very far from himself, because without Phil this story doesn't exist. Benedict himself is a polite, kind, woman-loving kind of man, but he's also a damn gifted actor. He was open to the psyche work I did. It became very important for entering deeply into the character, and you can see in the work there is no Benedict there."

JANE CAMPION

"When I first met Kodi, really the moment he walked through the door I started interviewing him as if he were Peter. He picked straight up and wove his own complex, curious philosophies into Peter's worldview. We spoke about his mother, his life in a tiny forgotten town, his ambitions for himself as a doctor and his ideas about how to control his destiny. I thought, 'We have not just found a smart Peter, we've got a Peter who is going to be more mercurial and mysterious than the character in the book.' "

JANE CAMPION

"When we started, I may have felt uncomfortable with the challenges Jane put on me, to push the boundaries I've used since I was nine years old in the industry. In rehearsals, I just completely let go. It's not only brought this character to life in a way I couldn't have done by myself but every character I will play after this. She's passionate about the process, about the dance of making it. Not just getting through it. She's passionate about it every step of the way."

KODI SMIT-McPHEE

"I remember saving an email from Jane, who wrote me about possibly working together—I think it was in 2001. So it was always a dream of mine. As a lover of film and filmmakers, she was always at the top of my list. Jesse was offered the role of George, and I was like, 'Wow, you're so lucky. You have to do this movie!' Then later I remember Facetiming with her for the first time with bated breath. And she says, 'Will you play my Rose?' I was so excited. It was truly a longtime dream come true."

KIRSTEN DUNST

"The script is a sensitive and compelling exploration of the battle between sexuality, masculinity and the closet. I feel it's incredibly timely as we continue to dissect the meaning and power associated with male and queer representation in cinema, the past and contemporary life."

IAIN CANNING

"Jane and I have known each other for over thirty years, and I feel incredibly lucky to have developed that relationship early on in her career. I would do anything for Jane, any kind of role."

GENEVIEVE LEMON

"Her focus and dedication trickles all the way through the crew, down to hair and makeup and wardrobe—every department. She has everything laid out in her mind, and the trick for a director is to get that outside of their mind and in front of their collaborators, to externalize it for others. That's the first step of collaborating, and then it's about giving everyone space to explore that. And it's not about being absolute, either. Like any artist who is honest about the process, she'll go from knowing exactly what she wants to admitting that she isn't sure, which is important because it leaves her open and willing to be surprised. Personally, I appreciate that. She's observant and focused when she's on set or when we're rehearsing, and there are little things that she'll pick up visually that you might be doing, and we'll build together as we find our way into the scenes."

JESSE PLEMONS

"Kirsten is the most open, gorgeous woman, and I immediately loved her. She says everything she's thinking. She's an open book. Her work is so honest, which makes it easy for me, but it couldn't have been easy for her, playing a suppressed 1925 woman where it's been culturally imprinted on Rose to be lesser than—to try and be sweet and pretty and always be pleasant. That is everything Kirsten has struggled against."

JANE CAMPION

"In rehearsal I wanted to start the two brothers off in a way that would bypass their brains and get them sensing into each other's energies. I thought dancing together might be a way, and I asked NZ choreographer Ross McCormack to teach Ben and Jesse a dance. Ross chose a waltz, as it brings them close. Ben had to lead, as he is the dominant brother, and Jesse had to learn to listen and follow. I made a little scenario that somewhat mimicked the power dynamics of the brothers in the first part of the story, Phil dominating and Jesse submitting but then with no warning Jesse peeling away and sitting down."

JANE CAMPION

PSYCHE WORK

"The challenge of directing, and the freedom, is to open up to whatever is in a project that you can bring all your discernment, all your psyche and all your dreams to. I did a lot of psyche work with Kim Gillingham. The psyche speaks in riddles, and Kim facilitates you penetrating them. She worked my dreams and said, 'Now, if you were Phil, what would you say to Jane?' 'Oh, she's a lightweight. She's standing back a long way. Tell her to get dirty. If she wants to know the story, she's got to be prepared to get really close and filthy.' I remember thinking he's right. I mean he (and I) is right. It's not enough to sit on the edge."

JANE CAMPION

The Cattle, photographed by Michael Crouser.
Opposite: Black Breeding Stallion, photographed by Charles Van Schaick.

Clockwise from top left: Brenner family photo, suspected inspiration for Bronco Henry. Brenner family photo, suspected inspiration for Phil Burbank. Brenner family photo. *Hat on Knee, Bell Ranch*, photographed in New Mexico by Bank Langmore, 1974. *Opposite: Cattle Roundup*, photographed by Grey Villet, 1960.

Clockwise from top left: Annemarie Schwarzenbach, photographed by Marianne Breslauer;
cowboy "dance stag," circa 1910; *Mountain Ranch*, by Michael Crouser; *Six Males, Nude, Wrestling*,
by Thomas Eakins, circa 1883.
Opposite: *Ryder 5*, by Michael Crouser, 2012.

High school rodeo rider, Topeka, Kansas, photographed by Jim Richardson.
Opposite: Mountain Farm, Rappahannock County, Virginia, by Arthur Rothstein, January 1940.

"Evelyn Cameron was a photojournalist recording what life was like in Montana in more or less the time period that our film takes place. She had a very good eye for landscape and placed her characters in front of huge landscapes, which was an incredible reference for all of us early on."

GRANT MAJOR, *production designer*

Moonrise at Shearer's Quarters, by Grahame Sydney, oil on linen, 840 x 1,215 mm, 2014.
Opposite: Four Men in Chaps: Jack Elliott, Floyd Carroll, Dean Thompson and J. P. Coats.

THE ROPE

Jane Campion

Before the start of shooting, all of the heads of departments were gathered so we could all have a final moment to talk about what we were going to do, how everyone would bring a part of themselves to the work. Then off we'd go into the day-to-day work. I wrote a piece about the rope, the push and pull of the story, and read it out loud to the group.

There's a lot of mythic work in this story. One of the talismans is this rope Phil is plaiting that he's going to give Peter and represented their relationship and what had to be hidden about it. We are careful to show the stages of making the rope within the story. It's such a good metaphor for our story and why I think the story is so damn clever. We have our four characters, and there are four different strands that you have to plait together to make the rope.

As the director it's my job to enter the story deeply to make sure it is enlivened from the blood, the guts, the bones up; to bring my imagination to each character individually and to look beyond the present moment of the story to where in each character's life, their pain, yearning, humanity their character was formed and how it figures now in the life of the story.

I start with my curiosity but this is not enough, a story like POWER OF THE DOG demands everything — I must meet my characters where they live. I cannot peer, poke or prod from the outside or they will not yield to me and the work will be flat and shallow. I have to meet them with my own grief, love, pain, with everything that I am and that they are.

Our story is set amidst extraordinary space, an ocean of space, in the sky and on the land, between the Ranch and the towns, between ~~from~~ one person and another.

Amidst this space there is the unusual togetherness of the brothers, Phil and George. Why, where there is so much space, in the house, on the land do they still cleave together? What makes George after all this time seperate from Phil?

It's not known. But what we do know is that by the time George brings Rose home as his wife, ~~the story is~~ the trouble has begun and the story is set in motion.

The story, it's shape, the way it unfolds and travels through time is THE CONTAINER.

"The transcendental will come of it's own accord when the container is strong enough"
Marion Woodman

So what is the transcendant? It's that which surpasses the normal or physical human experience. It's the great, deep, high reach of the story beyond the sum of it's parts. It's the capacity to awaken the psyche, to stimulate and enliven the soul. "When in doubt strengthen the container"

The container is the story structure but I also see it as the world building of the film. By in large, the choice of locations, the designs of the building, and rooms within the buildings, to make one believable world. ~~also including the cast, every living being in the story, the animals and what the characters are~~ wearing everyone wears where this story takes place. ~~A world~~

A world that will be memorable and whole. ~~A world where are~~ With a cast costumed to define and illuminate them-

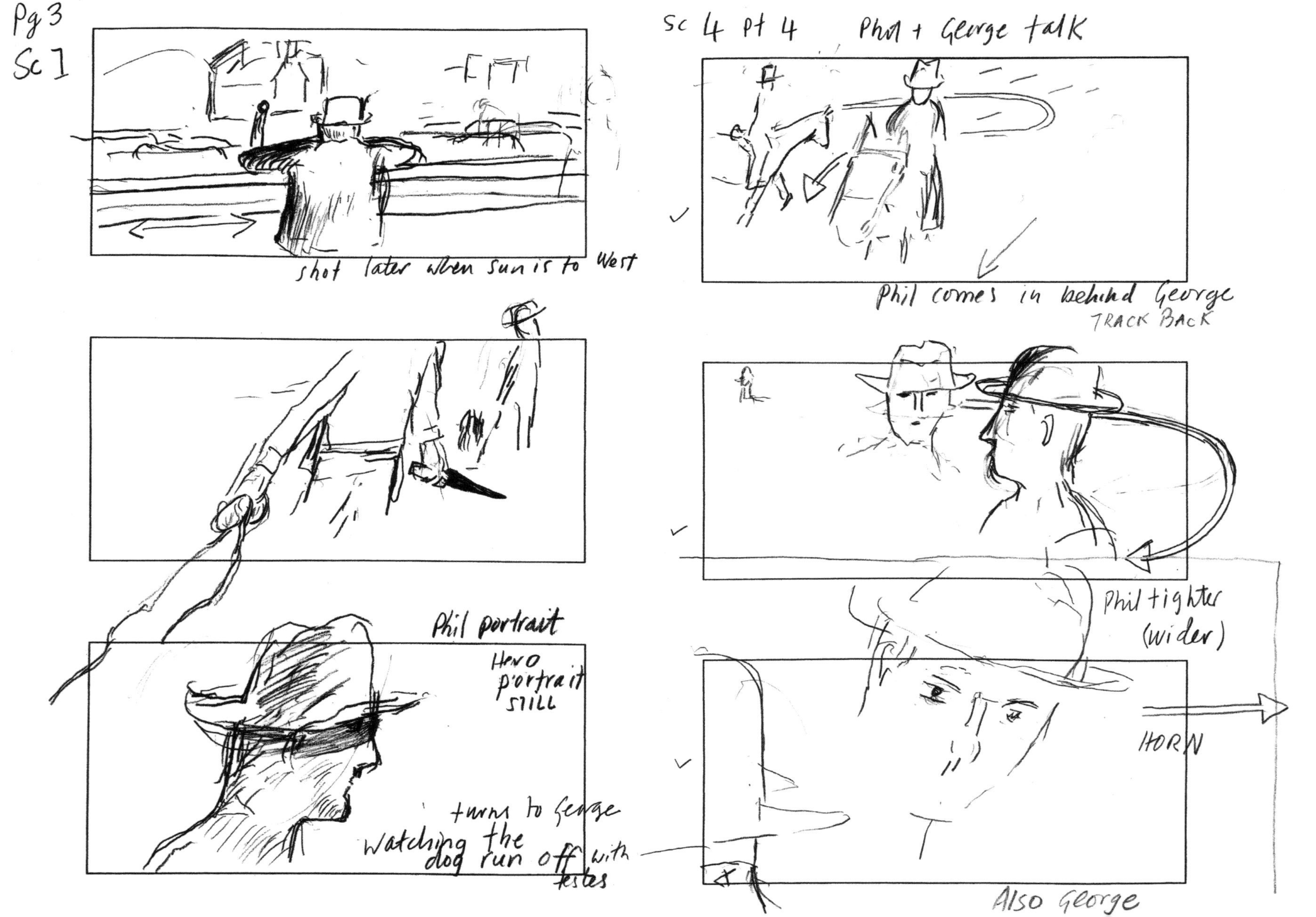

Pg 3
Sc 1

shot later when sun is to West

Sc 4 Pt 4   Phil + George talk

Phil comes in behind George
TRACK BACK

Phil portrait

Hero
portrait
STILL

turns to George
watching the
dog run off with
testes

Phil tighter
(wider)

HORN

Also George

sc 4 pt 5   — Car tipping to side

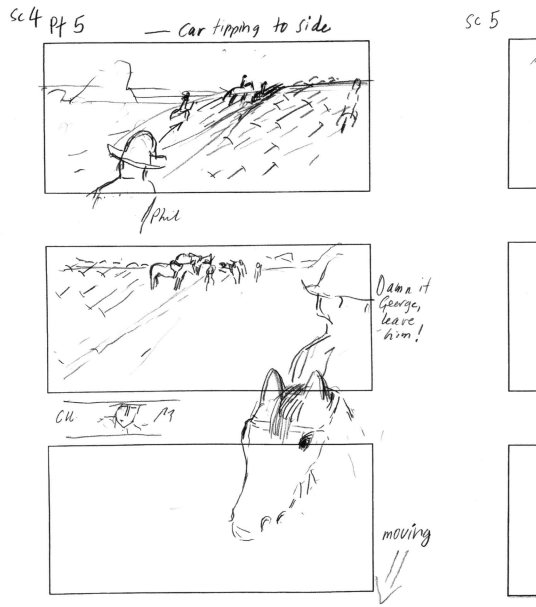

Phil

Damn it
George,
leave
him!

CU.

moving

sc 5

Peter working on his flowers
SLOW simple track.

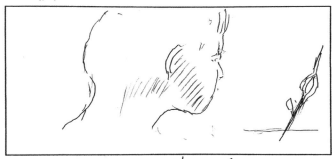

Strange flowers
unknown ones

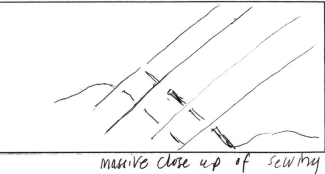

massive close up of sewing

Within the container I look for the images the symbols that need to be noticed, pulled out, paid attention to.

this The POWER OF THE DOG grows itself like a rope, a plaited, rawhide rope or the rope with which Peter's father hung himself and he, the Peter the son, cut him down.

Rope can make all sorts of shapes, lasso's, hangmen nooses, figures of eight. It can tie things together like calves to the horn of a saddle when it's time to brand or castrate or both. It can help you escape, save your life like the thick fire rope with the knots tied in it at the Red Mill so you can let yourself down from the top floor to the ground in case of fire.

The lariat, the rope that Phil crafts with his clever hands at the haymaking and decides to give to Peter is rich with consequence and meaning. A lariat is a rope designed for lasooing, for catching calves or horses or perhaps in Phil's case a y boy.

this rope, Phil's rope is made infront of us though we barely notice!

The cow that is hung and skinned (as George drives off, yet again, to his suicide widow") This hide is stripped from an animal arown and raised on their land.

ground ~~them~~. The skin heavy with fat is hung over ~~the~~ the corral fence to dry and ~~later~~ be processed. Magpies land on it ~~and~~ picking the flesh off it.

Next the skin is stretched, nailed up on the barn wall and later the hair scraped ~~and soaked~~ off it.

Once the skins are clean Phil cuts the skins ~~into~~ strips, a process I want us to see when George talks to Phil about 'washing' for the Governor's dinner. These strips are cut in a circular pattern around the outside edge of the skin and create the threads that the rope will be plaited from.

The weave of the rope is like the braiding of the story, the threads of Rose, George, Phil & Peter bending in and out of the story, the old Lady and Old Gent are finer threads added in for colour and punctuation.

But 'ROPE' in Peter's world has a darkness. It did not save his father's life but ended it. This darker message is already inside him when Peter collects an infected skin — in case, in case he needs it, in case he can use it. Rose has given away the other skins needed for finishing the rope. The rope is now literally tieing itself into the story.

miraculously the moment comes.

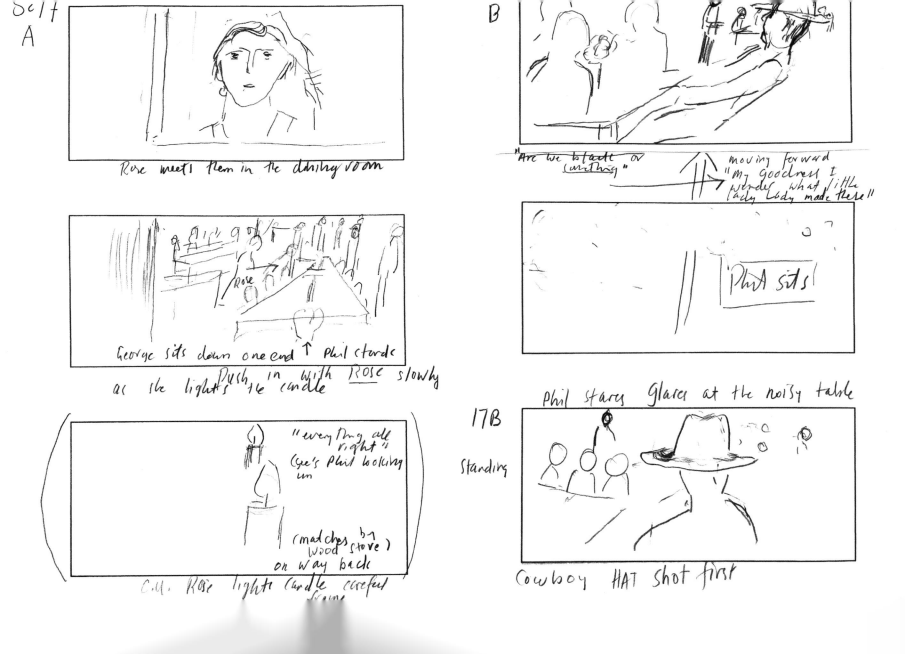

Sc/1
A

Rose meets them in the dining room

George sits down one end ↑ Phil stands
Push in with Rose slowly
as she lights the candle

"everything all
right"
(see's Phil looking
up

(matches by
wood stove)
on way back
C.U. Rose lights candle careful
frame

B

"Are we black or
something"

moving forward
"my goodness I
wonder what little
lady Lady made there"

Phil sits

Phil stares Glares at the noisy table

17B

Standing

Cowboy HAT shot first

Sc 57

Phil looking at Bronco's shrine

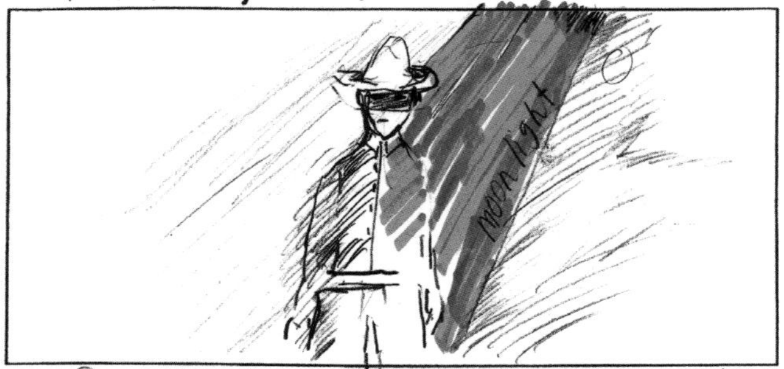
moonlight

Pacing here smoking then he rips the blanket off stands back

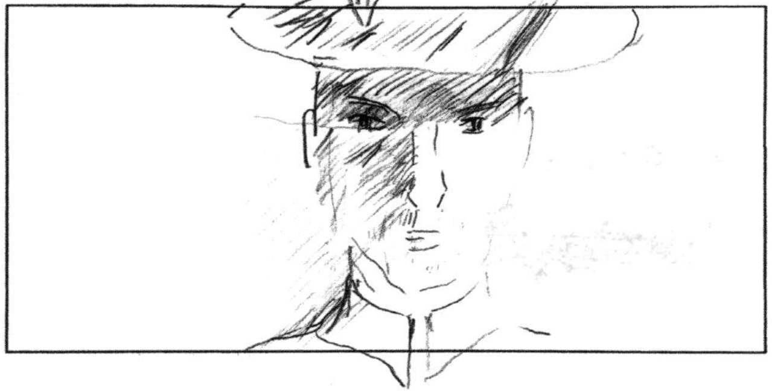

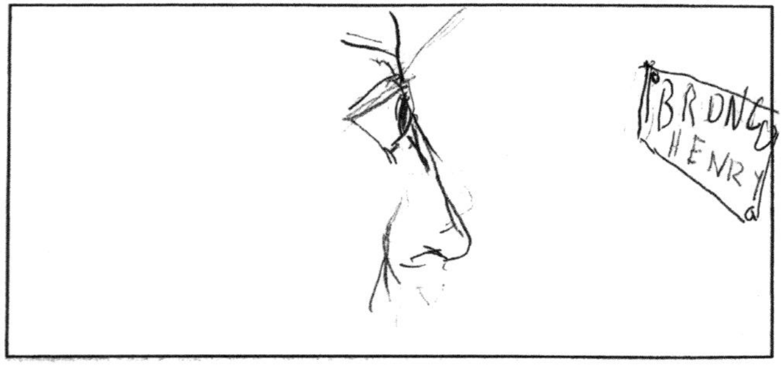
BRONCO
HENRY

could Be Profile if too similar to BARN

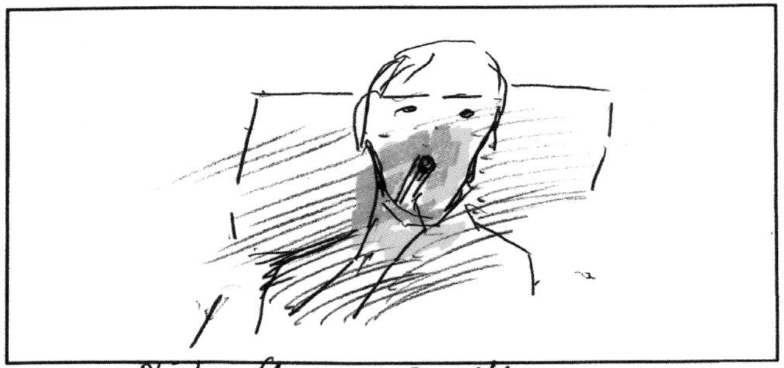

Phil after sex smoke

clear the room.

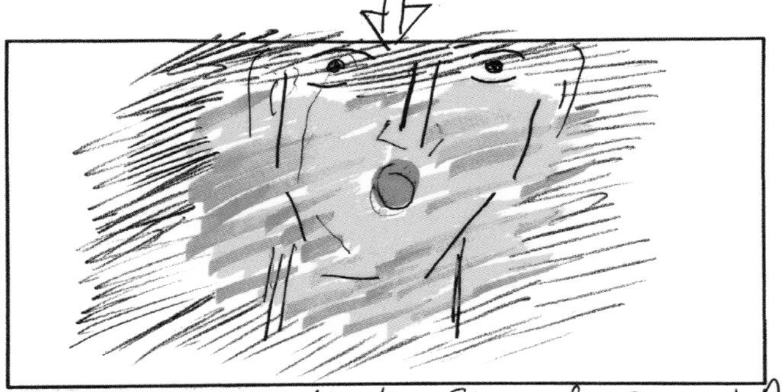

* Phil listens to the SEX of George + Rose but perhaps it's the talking the connectedness after that GETS Phil, makes his heart ache.

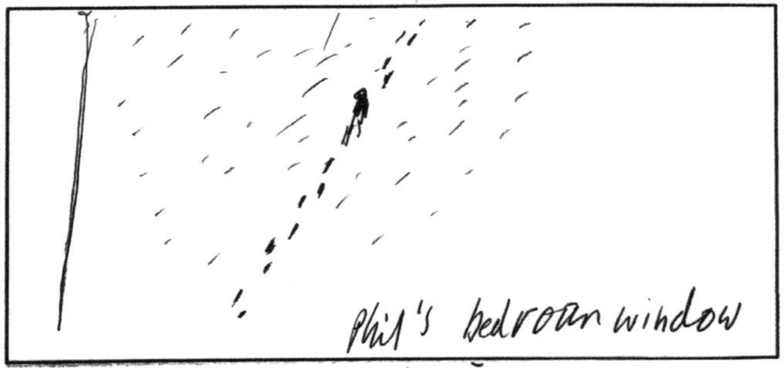
Phil's bedroom window

Push IN

The skin Peter offers Phil is found far out on the ranch from a dead cow bleeding from it's nose, an animal Phil would never normally touch. But in the heat of the moment, a very hot moment when Peter puts his hand on Phil's arm, Phil's guard is down, he believes the boy cares for him as he has come to care for the boy.

The making of the last metre of the rope is the climatic ending of the film. A love scene, a sex scene and a poisoning. The rope, the snake growing between Phil's legs is charged for sex and death.

The mood in the barn that night is tense with anticipation, their goals could not be more different. Phil wants love Peter to kill.

All the while the cut, the broken rope of Peter's father's suicide is being made whole.

The next day feverish with Anthrax poisoning, Phil leaves for the hospital. Where is the boy? Phil is waiting for Peter to come, perhaps even drive to the hospital. Phil, the finished rope in hand finally asks George "Where's the boy" George reassures Phil he will give him the rope. Now the cycle of the rope is almost complete. It means everything, but nothing as well. It's a talisman that winds us back to the beginning of the story. Made from this land, from a cow, but plaited and woven into a sophisticated object mirroring all the complexity and cleverness of the human heart and mind. It's what humans do, craft things ~~like to rope~~ then the ~~rope~~ things, the rope do things back like hang them or in Phil's case poison him.

Death by anthrax is not ~~as~~ certain ~~as the book would have it~~ at all. It must have been a nail biting moment for Peter. If Phil survives Peter and Rose's time at the ranch will be over, Phil will have put 2 + 2 together and Peter and his mother will be back to poverty.

As Phil's remains are lowered into the ground, (those ropes again) Peter who did not go to the funeral plays like a kid with Phil's dog. Later he reads Psalm 22 one Peter expects they might have read at Phil's graveside.

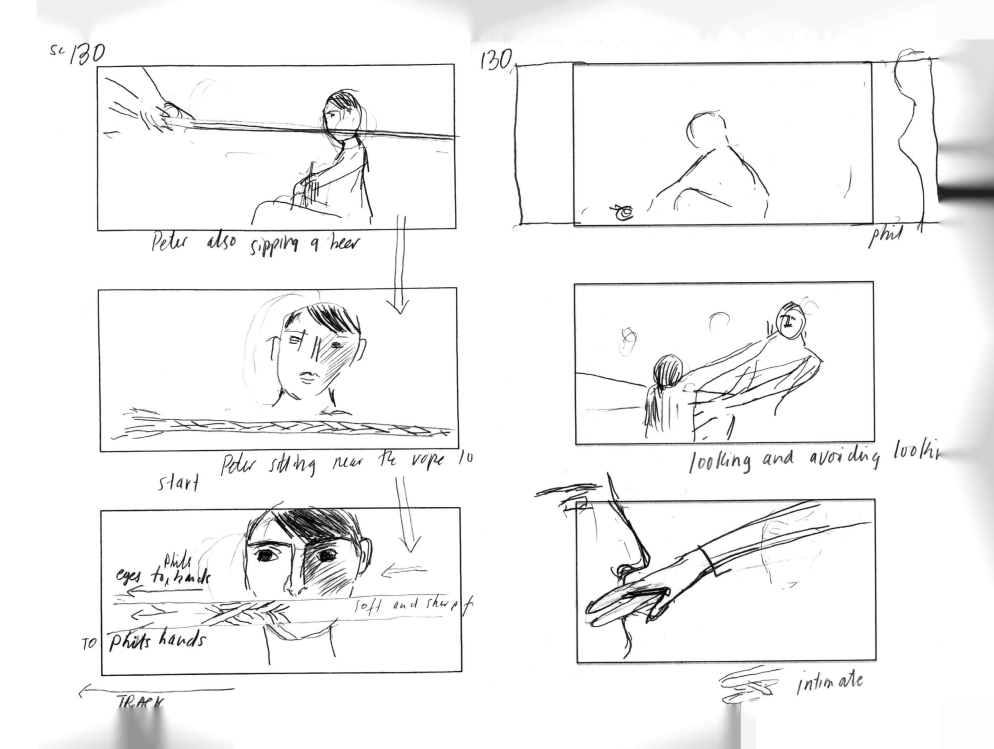

sc 130

Peter also sipping a beer

start   Peter sitting near the rope 10

Phils
eyes to hands

TO Phils hands

soft and sharp

TRACK

130,

phil

looking and avoiding looki

intimate

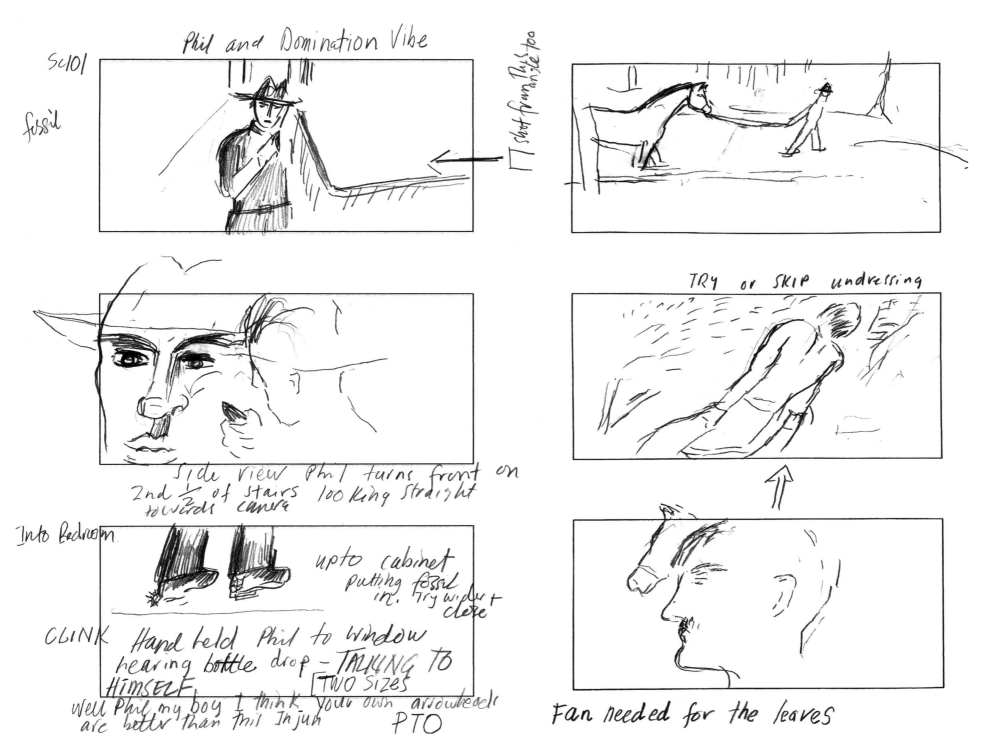

Phil and Domination Vibe

Sc101

fossil

IT shot from this side too

Side view Phil turns front on 2nd ½ of stairs looking straight towards camera

Into Bedroom

upto cabinet putting fossil in. Try w/dirt + clean

TWO SIZES

CLINK Hand held Phil to window hearing bottle drop — TALKING TO HIMSELF

Well Phil my boy I think your own arrowheads are better than this Injun

PTO

TRY or SKIP undressing

Fan needed for the leaves

Storyboards by Jane Campion.

THE PLAYERS

"Jane likes a lot of rehearsal and we improvise to get the energies of our roles together, but there are times where I'd rather hold back the emotion in the scene itself for filming. If I give all my emotion to it already, by the time we do it I'm over it in a weird way. Jane and I did work really hard on the heart scene with blocking, positioning and laying out on the couch: It almost felt like it was Rose's own little play, and it was important that we really got those beats down properly, for me to be able to be emotionally open."

KIRSTEN DUNST

"Then there is Jesse Plemons's masterfully understated performance as brother George. George's unexpected marriage motivates the plot, but his failure to see the danger to his new bride of being left in Phil's contemptuous, cruel orbit unlocks the need for her son, Peter, to step in and save her in his place."

TANYA SEGHATCHIAN

"One of the most thrilling parts of the filmmaking for me was being with Benedict when he's really sharing delicacy or revealing some vulnerability in the story and just being there with a camera that could get right in there. I see it as my job to try and create the atmosphere where it can live."

JANE CAMPION

"Kirsten's performance as Rose pulls on your heartstrings. It's impossible not to watch the film and feel for her and understand her and those situations. I think Jane and Kirsten's work together shows how frightening, intimidating and complex it would be to move into the Burbank house."

IAIN CANNING

"Jane's been incredibly sensitive about leading me into a place where I feel vulnerable and at ease. She knows what it is to go there, and she's very considerate, concerned and caring. She offers a huge amount of support for process and preparation, and really encourages and facilitates it, unlike any director I've ever worked with before. It's a very loving relationship that she has with her actors. She understands what they're risking in what they're trying to do. She's not afraid of her own vulnerabilities, and she encourages that in people in order to find something that's unexpected."

BENEDICT CUMBERBATCH

"George is called 'fatso' by Phil and mocked as being dumb, but George has the intelligence and kindness to find his way to happiness. The connection George and Rose find is very innocent and touching. On the hill, when Rose teaches George to dance, George says, 'I'm not alone anymore.' When you meet someone you love it is a very treasured emotion, and they express it perfectly."

JANE CAMPION

"Kodi Smit-McPhee's Peter excels in disarming us. The strange boy without fear who pursues his dreams and his curiosity in a world of blood and guts and machismo—indifferent to the humiliation and retribution his independence provokes in others."

"Peter's mother, Rose, the suicide widow, whose unlikely second chance as a future Mrs. Burbank is so delicately captured by Kirsten Dunst's nuanced performance of a powerless and lonely woman, having to oppress herself until the bottle becomes both her sole companion and the motor for her final act of defiance against her tormentor's dominance on the ranch. Everyone in the film is operating from a place of yearning, desire or grief.... All of them harbor secrets and hidden love, and those secrets inevitably unlock tension and surprises."

TANYA SEGHATCHIAN

"The story of women in film is sad *but* getting better and, as I've quipped before, more of a haiku than a history. I love women, I believe in equal rights, I am a feminist and I am an artist. It has been my passion to fall in love with female characters and tell their stories. While they're not the only stories I've told, all of my work is through my eye, a female eye. When I fell in love with this story, I felt curious that this time it was a male protagonist—and what a guy! I have a particular thing for alphas. They are so damn ugly and tragic and lonely and make life hell for everyone else and in the animal world tend to have a short and violent life."

"Working with Benedict, Kirsten, Jesse and Kodi, I felt we got beyond gender differences to a more expansive place, which is loving and knowing each other and really supporting the effort and intelligence everyone was bringing to the work. We were just humans working at our capacity, bringing everything we could to it. Communication was important to us all, and we made efforts to keep it flowing."

JANE CAMPION

SHUTDOWN

Jane Campion

Like everywhere else in the world, when the pandemic arrived in New Zealand, it arrived like a lightning storm. Within a week, really. We'd just finished all our exteriors, and I was thinking, "Oh God, what could go wrong now? It's so great—now we're just in a studio. It's going to be super-simple." When two or three people with Covid appeared in New Zealand, we were saying, "Two or three? That's nothing." But every day they kept multiplying, and I felt like my responsibility was to just try to keep things genuinely safe and at the same time be strategic about trying to finish shooting the people who came from overseas, like the Old Lady and the Governor. You're thinking, "God, it's going to be so hard to get those people back." We just managed to shoot them and then we had to close down, and the country was closed down the day after.

I was in shock for the first day or two. I just kind of slept and rested, and then I thought I've got to come to terms with the fact that this may be over for us now. We may never get to shoot this. Benedict has to go on to other films after this. So, for a while, I just accepted that maybe it was over. And I was quite surprised how well I took that. But as time went on, I realized that—in New Zealand, at least—the Covid numbers were coming round to zero and that we looked like we could probably set up the film.

I started campaigning the government to let our actors and crew back in and talked to Benedict about starting up again, because he was still in New Zealand with his family, which was lucky for them and for us. And I think we were one of the first shoots back up. Covid did have some perverse benefits for all of us. It gave us a rest, a chance to drop more deeply into what we were doing and think about it, get some more perspective. I went back a little more grateful. You just felt everything was more precious and everybody there was more precious.

PRODUCTION DESIGN

"The house is central in the production design of the film. It's this iconic family presence that's on the land. Our notion of the house's construction period is roughly 1880 to 1885. The parents would've come to Montana from the eastern areas of maybe New York or Chicago and brought with them their hifalutin city ideas of house aesthetics. We chose a very early Arts and Crafts style for the house and based it on the sort of things that we could find. There's a very famous house in America called Sagamore Hill, which is where President Roosevelt used to live, that we looked at for inspiration."

GRANT MAJOR

Concept art by Liam Beck.
Opposite: Production designer Grant Major.

"It was always a consideration to shoot in New Zealand, even though the film is set in Montana. Jane is from New Zealand and of that landscape. We were naturally nervous. Was it going to feel authentic? We did some tests on Americans, asking, 'Which photo is New Zealand, and which one's Montana?' People couldn't guess."

EMILE SHERMAN

"I remember the first time driving up on the South Island to the Burbank-ranch set and walking in it. I was blown away. No one should tear it down. It was masterful. Grant Major is so special, thinking about every little thing you see on set and giving it a sense of history and story."

KIRSTEN DUNST

Top: Concept art by Liam Beck.

December 17, 2018: Found the ranch-house location in Otago, New Zealand, beneath the Hawkdun Range.

November 25, 2019: Barn construction starts.

December 19, 2019: Ranch-house construction starts.

Set construction on the three-story ranch house and the barn took months to
complete. In addition to the set construction, the team had to age the sets to look like
they were built in 1885 and then aged forty more years, as the film takes place in 1925.
Principal photography began on January 23, 2020.

"Phil and George's parents had moved out of the Burbank ranch twenty years beforehand, taking a quantity of furniture with them, and in our minds the rooms haven't really changed from that moment. It's a nice parallel with the slightly empty lives of George and Phil when we come to them in the story. Phil and George don't use the house the way it was first intended."

GRANT MAJOR

"Jane and I worked together thirty years ago on *An Angel at My Table*. I truly respect Jane's intelligence and sensitivity. She's one of Australasia's best directors, probably one of the world's best directors, in my view. She really knows what she's doing, and she's got a really good eye for production design. It's a little unusual, in many ways, to go into the level of detail together that we did, and we worked quite intensely laying out the ranch in terms of its geography. She doesn't make her mind up easily. She likes to keep things fluid for as long as she can, so you're trying all these different options that she likes to have in front of her to find the very best solution. When I first read the script, it felt like a classic 1960s-1970s Hollywood film: big, epic, set on a cattle ranch with all these very masculine people populating it. On a second read I got down into the dynamics of the characters, and their interactions were incredibly powerful. It's beautifully written. I still claim that it's the best script I've ever read."

GRANT MAJOR

"Grant can do the really big things, but we also had to make a journal for the Peter character, which was a wish book for how they would get themselves out of their one-trick-pony town. People were stepping around this project because it was going to be hard to make a journal we all really loved. Finally, Grant took it on, and the feminine side of Grant just completely came out, how he cut around the pictures. Really decorating the edges of it. It was so incredibly decorative and amazing. It wasn't like building the ranch house. It was a boy's, effeminate boy's, journal. And it was perfect. Inspiring."

JANE CAMPION

CINEMATOGRAPHY

"Ari Wegner, our director of photography, is a star. She is true and constant, intelligent, poetic and hardworking. She also honestly looks about twelve years old, perhaps because every morning before work she runs an hour. Her nature is kind, and she is always focused, though enjoys a laugh. Very importantly she handholds like an angel, syncing deeply into the actor's energy. Like me she likes a long preparation. We both know we can offer a project and ourselves much more if we have the time to properly dig deep and together find the right photographic language for the story—as simple, elegant, intimate and direct as we can make it. For Ari and myself, the story is our guide and our strength. Showy visual flourishes have no place. Ari's instinct for story and character development is like a writer's. She is endlessly curious about how best to reveal character and story. We spent so much time together planning and preparing—our brains felt co-joined. We fretted about all the things we could not control: extreme weather with winds so strong you had to take shelter, the river drying up, the river flooding, the grass not being blond enough, no wet-weather cover. The one thing that did come our way we could never have imagined—Covid-19."

JANE CAMPION

"Just before Jane started rehearsals, she and I spent a month together, away from the world, just planning. We went to stay in Central Otago, storyboarding and then testing our plans in the locations. Lots of driving and talking about the script and exploring the property where we shot, finding angles and vantage points, getting to understand the light on the mountain range."

"Shooting in New Zealand is a wonderful experience. It's a landscape that gives so much. I think it might be something to do with the geology and the geography of the land, but there's a way in New Zealand that you can see mountains that is hard in some other places. That part of the world [New Zealand] is so rural and so sparsely populated that we were also able to re-create a world where there were no power lines, no freeways, no factories. It's a 360 place that hasn't changed for a long time."

ARI WEGNER

"I first became aware of Jane's work when I was in high school in media class. Our media teacher showed us *Peel* and *Passionless Moments*, and I was just captivated by this humor but also a really true, honest observation that wasn't judgmental and had a curiosity, but also had a kind of rigor and a strictness of the language. That mixture is something that makes you pay attention. On set, Jane is a fabulous mix of incredibly focused and incredibly fun. We all do our best work when we're at ease, and we do our most interesting work and the most surprising work, and we're prepared to take risks. There's no fear. Which is really different to most film sets, which can be quite stressful. But I think for her there's a difference between high pressure and high stress. It has to be fun as well, otherwise why are we here? That's an amazing energy to have leading the team. It's important that there's silliness and nothing's taken too seriously. She also has this youthful curiosity about the world, which I think allows her to see things that many people overlook, but when we see them on-screen, we recognize them and they resonate."

ARI WEGNER

COSTUME DESIGN

"Meeting Kirsty Cameron, our costume designer, was like meeting a soul sister. Her whole being is completely caught up in how to bring this story alive. How to help the characters feel themselves and how to control the palette. She had the reins very firmly in her hands."

JANE CAMPION

Costume designer Kirsty Cameron.

"Jane comes at the story and the characters from a subterranean place of exploration. Connecting to the story on a deep level, she brings her own life and experience to the emotional life of the characters and to the story, plus a profound understanding of what the film needs. Jane is also very open, inclusive and present when you communicate with her, and there's an inspirational spark that passes through you, or between you, in these moments."

KIRSTY CAMERON

HOW AT
ODDS with the
PINK ROOM
IS, SHE

CONTRAST
THE LANDSCAPE
THE DARK HOUSE
THE PINK ROOM

TOO DELICATE
FOR THE
LANDSCAPE

PINK
ROOM

HOW DOES
CHANGE
BEING

ROSE
rodeo shirt

authentically not
tricked up.
a little sexy. not
a baggy
collar/high up neck

FENDI

SHIRTS +
SWEATERS +
BLOUSES

WONKY
DRESSING

"I really fell in love with the sheepies, as they call them, which are the chaps with sheepskin on them, because everyone looks like satyrs. I think it's very sexy. I really love the fact that it was 1925, which gives it another sort of a twist. Cowboys were becoming quotable and were buying gear from catalogs. They're kind of catalog cowboys—even they were following cowboys in the movies at that point, because movies had begun."

JANE CAMPION

"We were working with some wonderful reference images that often contradicted the clichés of the time, especially in some of the homemade clothing. We weren't betrothed to period and in fact spoke of creating 'our own peculiar world.' This— combined with genuine surprises, like cowboys of the time wearing striped knitwear—meant we had the freedom to put tone, mood and character first."

"The characters are either set against the emptiness and monumentality of the landscape or the darkness of the house, and we decided to restrict the palette of each scene to five colors, not always the same colors. With this in mind, plus the austereness of the brothers' lives, the characters' costumes become partially an exercise in restraint."

KIRSTY CAMERON

Costume illustrations by Henrietta Harris for Kirsty Cameron.

SCORE

TO Jonny Greenwood

FROM Jane Campion

I very much hope you are good.

I wanted to share with you the Psalm that the title of our story comes from. It's a startling, brutal and intense cry out to the creator and while our Phil is no Jesus, there is an intensity of feeling in Phil. I believe this visceral intensity lives in the psyche of this material and could be part of the musical language of the film which by the way is what I already sense you are doing.

It feels to me like the full extreme of human suffering, humiliation and want.

"I am poured out like water, and all my bones are out of joint: my heart is like wax; it is melted in the midst of my bowels"

"Save me from the lion's mouth: for thou hast heard me from the horns of the unicorns"....

I know you were thinking of ideas for the ugly duet and if there are any further conversations you want or assistance from Tanya or Andrew please let me know.

Tanya gets back to London at the end of November and would love to meet up with you.

Best wishes,

Jane

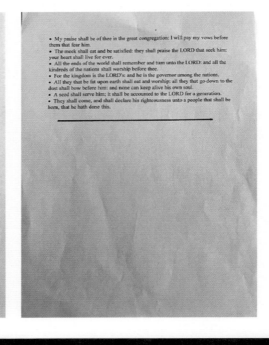

Psalm 22:20

My God, my God, why hast thou forsaken me? why art thou so far from helping me, and from the words of my roaring?

- O my God, I cry in the day time, but thou hearest not; and in the night season, and am not silent.
- But thou art holy, O thou that inhabitest the praises of Israel.
- Our fathers trusted in thee: they trusted, and thou didst deliver them.
- They cried unto thee, and were delivered: they trusted in thee, and were not confounded.
- But I am a worm, and no man; a reproach of men, and despised of the people.
- All they that see me laugh me to scorn: they shoot out the lip, they shake the head, saying,
- He trusted on the LORD that he would deliver him: let him deliver him, seeing he delighted in him.
- But thou art he that took me out of the womb: thou didst make me hope when I was upon my mother's breasts.
- I was cast upon thee from the womb: thou art my God from my mother's belly.
- Be not far from me; for trouble is near; for there is none to help.
- Many bulls have compassed me: strong bulls of Bashan have beset me round.
- They gaped upon me with their mouths, as a ravening and a roaring lion.
- I am poured out like water, and all my bones are out of joint: my heart is like wax; it is melted in the midst of my bowels.
- My strength is dried up like a potsherd; and my tongue cleaveth to my jaws; and thou hast brought me into the dust of death.
- For dogs have compassed me: the assembly of the wicked have inclosed me: they pierced my hands and my feet.
- I may tell all my bones: they look and stare upon me.
- They part my garments among them, and cast lots upon my vesture.
- But be not thou far from me, O LORD: O my strength, haste thee to help me.
- Deliver my soul from the sword; my darling from the power of the dog.
- Save me from the lion's mouth: for thou hast heard me from the horns of the unicorns.
- I will declare thy name unto my brethren: in the midst of the congregation will I praise thee.
- Ye that fear the LORD, praise him; all ye the seed of Jacob, glorify him; and fear him, all ye the seed of Israel.
- For he hath not despised nor abhorred the affliction of the afflicted; neither hath he hid his face from him; but when he cried unto him, he heard.

- My praise shall be of thee in the great congregation: I will pay my vows before them that fear him.
- The meek shall eat and be satisfied: they shall praise the LORD that seek him: your heart shall live for ever.
- All the ends of the world shall remember and turn unto the LORD: and all the kindreds of the nations shall worship before thee.
- For the kingdom is the LORD's: and he is the governor among the nations.
- All they that be fat upon earth shall eat and worship: all they that go down to the dust shall bow before him: and none can keep alive his own soul.
- A seed shall serve him; it shall be accounted to the LORD for a generation.
- They shall come, and shall declare his righteousness unto a people that shall be born, that he hath done this.

TO   Jane Campion

FROM   Jonny Greenwood

Hi Jane,

I'm experimenting at the moment with the pianola ideas, principally looking at ways to introduce imperfections and mechanical stutters/distortions into the midi which is sent to the piano. Lots of programming nights ahead (a good thing....) and perhaps this is something that can recur, with increasing chaos, at the close of each act. Or else other types of treatments to suggest the building fate. I don't know - but I do have confidence that the mechanical piano will be worth trying. It can be prepared too, a la Cage, which makes it more of a percussion thing (I think Cecil Taylor described the piano as '88 tuned drums') - so again, a whole world to explore with this thing.

Are you still thinking of shooting black and white? Perhaps you've reconsidered, but I was into the idea: something about pin-sharp black and white really burrows in. Anyway - I'm colour-blind, so not one to give opinions!

Other thoughts, all pretty nebulous, still:

- I wonder why the banjo hasn't been used in contemporary classical music (aside from a few George Crumb ensembles) and certainly never as a solo instrument. There's probably a good reason we'll soon find out...in any case, I do want to try thinking in terms of string chamber music with a banjo - but perhaps material that is more atonal than necessarily idiomatic to the banjo. It can be a violent sound.

- Also - another thought - perhaps strings are too safe. I did think that the screenplay suggested, rather, brass. Principally French horns / trumpets - not in a jazz sense, but a romantic 20th century kind of way. I'm uncertain because (a) this is all a bit moot without any footage, and (b) I'm partly motivated by wanting to use brass instead of (just) strings, which in itself is probably unwise, as I've not written much in that world. Anyway, like I say, just something about the script, and reinforced by your talk of repressed passion and pain. French horns are exactly that, to me. Sad repression that turns to anger as the volume increases. Bassoons too. Maybe a wind ensemble. I could send you some wind ensemble recordings?

- And - the 'standard' banjo material - I wondered if there was a way to form a little group, with banjo, string bass, harmonium, and 1920's drums:

But again, closer to the world of Tom Waits (in its production, at any rate) than anything too clean / shiny. T Bone Burnett is great, but - not like that.

This is all to put the cart/horse the wrong way round, as there's nothing visual yet - though I might as well be working on some of these over Christmas, even if it's just the software, which I like more and more as an idea. Midi is all about clean, careful reproduction. It'll be fun to make it do the opposite.

I've followed the Sydney fires - just terrible. I drove through all that between Sydney and Byron Bay when we lived in Darlinghurst. Can't believe it's destroyed an area so immense. Did your house survive?

Best wishes,
Jonny

TO   Jonny Greenwood

FROM   Jane Campion

Dearest Jonny,

Thank you for your patience, I am so happy we are all through the bureaucracy and very happy you are our composer. It's really a dream for me!

I just wanted to mention that when our story cuts to black, as it does a few times between acts, I have been thinking it's a moment to try marking with music some sense of the steps of fate as the story builds towards its crisis.... we don't know what it is but it's coming kind of idea..... makes me think of the impossibly fast victrola you sent us early on. Anyway it's all wide open for your inspiration and I'd love to hear anything you want to send. I find it better to get a suite of possible music going before the shoot so I can film thinking of it and start early on to lay it into the cut. I don't want to use temp music, much prefer using simple or trial versions of what might be in the end.

I hope you and Tanya have fun next week. Wish I was there.

My major note is the music in my mind gives voice to the unexpressed soul and passion and yearning psyche stuff -- deep, painful, beautiful.

Not much to ask ha ha!

Meanwhile in Sydney there are terrible fires. My holiday house by a river in the bush may be swallowed up. And in NZ where I am now, we are in flood conditions (my preference-- more Noah's ark stuff than hellfire fury) and there is nothing but rain in the next week in NZ. Those riding rivers....

Hope Winter proceeds mildly in Oxford.

I do hope we get to meet later in this process. Look forward to it.

Cheers, Jane xx

Hi Jane,

I saw Tanya on Monday, along with some selected scenes. It was very encouraging / inspiring. Of course it's hard to tell from a few clips (in terms of what music might work) but what's certain is there's great footage already. You've a very gifted DP.

So - I talked to Tanya about first approaches, and explained that finding the right instruments / ensembles etc would be a good start.

Musically, I think there's two questions: what sounds suit the landscape and colour, which I perhaps have more of a handle on now - and what is the tone of the relationships, and how the music can counterpoint that. Tanya suggests it's quite a sensual film (in amongst the castration / anthrax / alcoholism / hatred - all that good stuff) - so clearly there are contrasts to be enjoyed (musically as well) - and ambiguities too maybe.

I've suggested looking at using some slightly non-Hollywood tonalities. Contemporary music can be lyrical and beautiful without tipping into anything too traditional. I say 'contemporary' but really just mean post 1950 really. Though with the, for example, castration scene (assuming there's music there) we can maybe go further.

Perhaps this reads like a desire to just throw unlistenable noise at you - it isn't...I think I'm just responding to how contemporary the film looks: it's not nostalgic / retro / pastiche-y - so there's no reason for the music to be.

Peter seems to be a key character to explore musically. There's that definition of camp that Stephen Fry uses - that camp is synonymous with strong - which is true. And true in this story.

I also mentioned electronics to Tanya: maybe there's a way to augment traditional instruments with old (very old?) electronic sounds in a way that's more interesting: I'd like to use delayed / affected French Horn / Trumpet to describe the landscape. Normally this kind of big American landscape is sweeping strings - but that feels wrong.

I'm really just blathering. Apologies. Racing brain-gear looking for something to engage with - but mostly just making a noise.

First things first - I'll try and do a few piano demos, see what you respond to. With the brass, it's harder: there are samples, but they don't really give too much of an idea. Ditto the strings. But I can attempt a few.

Best wishes,
Jonny

"I'm lucky I got the chance to write and record this soundtrack: Jane was open-minded and very trusting, especially given that there were no real demos made of many of the ideas. The final recordings were often the first recordings. When I look back over our very first email exchanges (though, in fact, some are scanned handwritten notes, which is much nicer), it's interesting to chart what early ideas did prove fertile (French horns in reverb for the landscape shots, detuned mechanical pianos) and those which didn't (banjo as soloist in a twentieth-century-style classical string quartet, which was as bad an idea as it sounds)."

"The main thought I kept returning to was that this film is set in the modern era: it's too easy to assume any cowboy story is nineteenth century, and there is lots of culture in Phil's character. He's well read, and it's not hard to imagine his taste in music being—alongside his proficiency on the banjo— very sophisticated. The pleasure in a character this complex, and emotionally pent-up, is that it allows for complexity in some of the music, as well as simpler, sweeter things for his contrasting brother. Bouncing between these two characters, musically, generated a lot of ideas."

"In terms of the process, I remember there were some definite moments where progress was made. The banjo was a bit of a dead end, but it led to me learning to play the cello like a banjo and that was a productive technique. Similarly, the atonal piano, played by a machine, instantly made sense when put to picture. Elsewhere I had the fun of recording French horns in an enormous church in Oxford—the first time I've spent time with these remarkable instruments as solo voices. And there were some days with my favorite string players. These kinds of recording sessions always make me very happy. Throughout this, there was the gentle enthusiasm of Jane and her team—which was very inspiring, and all made for a really productive, enjoyable few months."

JONNY GREENWOOD

TO Jonny Greenwood

FROM Jane Campion

Dear Jonny,

So lovely to hear from you! Also delighted to know you were enjoying the footage you saw. I'm so IN IT on an everyday kind of way. I have lost all sense of what we are doing except to say trying our best!

As for what music would be best, I have only one answer—YOUR music; however, you feel inspired to try. I think no matter what instruments you land on, it's going to have your taste, complexity, modernism, lyricism, and feeling. Please keep blathering. I think all good things just begin somewhere and then with trust and faith build and evolve...so I think just making a noise is great, perfect.

I am hopeful we will begin to understand what works musically for this film by some good old trial and error. The piano demos sound like a good place to start.

I really hope you feel free and encouraged to experiment—I'll try to be as honest and open as possible.

Jane

"Jonny Greenwood, our composer, is a genius. Simple as that."

JANE CAMPION

HAIR & MAKEUP

"Noriko Watanabe is head of our hair and makeup, and I've done every single project with Noriko since *The Piano*, except for *Bright Star*. We have a wonderful relationship of really loving the journey together, and she's a wild woman, with a great deal of energy and imagination. She's very good at what she does. I fight with her like crazy about my versions of how that might be and how she could help me get there, and she fights me back with 'Not like this, like that.' But she always gets the best wigs, and we work it out in the end. It's a little mad, but we do it, and I love Noriko."

JANE CAMPION

"My vision is Jane's vision. She pays very particular attention to how each character looks and I follow her lead. Ever since we started working together on *The Piano* her vision changed on each film. That has been such a blessing for me as a hair and makeup designer. It's a gift to be continually challenged. There isn't a template and *The Power of the Dog* is no exception. I simply want to achieve the amazing vision she already has in her head and her heart."

NORIKO WATANABE

EDITING

"My approach was to really understand how Jane saw the story and characters before making too many judgments or jumping to too many conclusions. Immediately after reading the script, I knew it would be a film with incredibly complex characters and relationships, and I knew to truly start bringing it together I needed to understand Jane and try and see everything from her POV. There is so much between the lines in this film and so much humanity, and that is a complicated thing to express while keeping a focus on the story. We wanted to retain all the richness in the characters and relationships while keeping the story moving and building with momentum and tension, to find the perfect balance where the audience is leaning in for every glance and breath."

"We slowly revealed Phil's character and the secret he was keeping. There was a scene that revealed his sexuality more explicitly much earlier on which we chose to remove. It didn't feel right to express such a clear and simple explanation for his nature. It felt reductive of his characters heartbreak and pain. Cutting Peter's character was really interesting. It was crucial that he was hard to read. His reactions are often disarming and he seems to be detached, but it was equally important that the audience was aware of his internal emotional world and his great love for his mother. We wanted to really emphasize this early on in the film, before his arrival at the ranch. To me, he always felt like the most confident character, and even though in this world he is seen as weak, he has a great strength and sense of self."

PETER SCIBERRAS

"We really tried not to overuse the landscape. It always needed to have an emotional reason for being there and had to be earned. It was often about creating a sense of foreboding or to emphasize a feeling and allow space for the audience to sit with that feeling for a moment longer. One of my favorite moments is right after the funeral. We cut to the widest shot of the ranch we have seen. It's in beautiful light, and for the first time it feels small and peaceful, dwarfed by the powerful hills. Phil's reign is over."

PETER SCIBERRAS

"He loves the riddles of editing and thinking about it. He has this sweetness in him, a sense that we can do this, we can get through this, we'll work it out. We'll just keep going, and nothing's ever too much trouble. He's always ready and eager to get on to the next issue, next problem, and to solve it together."

JANE CAMPION

"The whole of filmmaking is trusting in the relationships you form. It's a big exercise in trust over doubt, inspiration over fear. It can be terrifying. You have to have 2 percent more inspiration and then you can manage, but if you have less than that, you stink. Fear in filmmaking is very real. It's normal. Many things can go wrong, and you always have to be thinking about what they are and how you can affect things to change that ratio."

JANE CAMPION

MY UNSUNG HEROES

Jane Campion

In every production there are my special heroes, without whose loyalty, talent, sensitivity, above-and-beyond dedication this film would not have been possible. My on-set husband and first assistant, Phil Jones, an actual film lover who can focus a set like no one's business and keeps me laughing and the set moving effortlessly. He believes in me more than I believe in me. My wonderful, deeply capable, talented, genius ladies of production, Libby Sharpe and Chloe Smith. I love these women. They are kind, and their knowledge is phenomenal. My dear personal assistants, Claire Van Beek and Toni Mager. These two humans, so talented in their own right and so caring and alert, keep me rested, fed, happy and upright . . . thank you, darlings. Tanya also thanks Drew Marshall for his looking out for her with humor and capacity. Rachel House, who did the acting preparation work with the cowhands—kind, funny, instinctive, brilliant.

There are many others to thank, but foremost Roger Frappier for giving me this opportunity. Emile Sherman and Iain Canning of See-Saw for loving the project and coming on board with all their care and smarts. Our wise adviser John Woodward ("Ask the PM"). So many helping, caring hands along the way, so helpful, so important: Anna and Michael Campion, my brother and sister, keeping it real, and Annabelle Sheehan, Rose Garnett, Kim Gillingham, Annie Proulx, Alan Weltzien. Also, those from Netflix who gave encouragement and feedback, Lisa Nishimura and Sean Berney, thank you.

Jane's assistant Claire Van Beek.

THE POWER

OF THE DOG

ACKNOWLEDGMENTS

Tanya Seghatchian, Libby Sharpe, Sam Joly, Tracey Mair, Kirsty Cameron, Lisa Taback, Lisa Bass, Marla Weinstein, Katie Doyle, Bianca Asnaran, Catherine Rinaldo, Kalie Watch, Steven Newman, Brittany Carr Seely and Christopher Gonzalez, who put this book together despite the ever-changing whims of Jane and Tanya.

CREDITS

Unit Photography by Kirsty Griffin; © 2021 Cross City Films Limited/Courtesy of Netflix.
Film Stills by Ari Wegner; © 2021 Cross City Films Limited/Courtesy of Netflix.

P. 199: (left) "Untitled" (Dog) © Giacomo Brunelli; (right) © Harold Mendez; p. 202: (left) All Rights Reserved; (right) Courtesy of Elizabeth Main/Photography by Addison Berkey; p. 216: Wisconsin Historical Society, WHI-(# 28603); pp. 217, 222: © Michael Crouser 2021 from the book *Mountain Ranch*; p. 220: (top row, bottom right) Brenner Family Archive; (bottom left) © Bank Langmore; p. 221: © Grey Villet/The LIFE Picture Collection/Shutterstock; p. 223 (top left) © Walter & Konrad Feilchenfeldt/Courtesy Fotostiftung Schweiz; (top right) All Rights Reserved; (bottom right) © Michael Crouser 2021 from the book *Mountain Ranch;* (bottom left) Photography by Thomas Eakins/ All Rights Reserved; p. 224: © Jim Richardson; p. 225: Library of Congress, Prints & Photographs Division, FSA/OWI Collection, [LC-USF347-029226-D]; p. 226: © Evelyn Cameron Heritage, Inc. All Rights Reserved; p. 228: "Moonrise at the Shearer's Quarters." Oil on Linen. 840 x 1215mm. 2014. Grahame Sydney. Grahamesydney.com; p. 229: Meyers Collection, B-916/2, Wyoming State Archives, [B-916/00002].

Every possible effort has been made to identify and contact all rights holders and obtain their permission for work appearing in these pages. Any errors or omissions brought to the publisher's attention will be corrected in future editions.

Slipcase: Kirsty Griffin.
Cover: Kirsty Griffin.

© 2021 Assouline Publishing
3 Park Avenue, 27th Floor
New York, NY 10016 USA
Tel: 212 989 6769 Fax: 212 647 0005
www.assouline.com

Printed in Italy by Grafiche Milani.
ISBN: 9781649800534